*Love!
Ange — ... ... N. MAN*

MW00861104

Misplaced

by
Angelina Wentz Memon

PublishAmerica
Baltimore

First printing

ISBN: 1-4241-6668-3
PUBLISHED BY PUBLISHAMERICA, LLLP
www.publishamerica.com
Baltimore

Printed in the United States of America

I would like to dedicate this book to all of the Amerasians who suffered through mental and physical torture in Vietnam and whose voices were never heard.

ACKNOWLEDGEMENTS

In memory of my beloved grandmother, who raised me to become the woman I am today.

In memory of my grandfather, who died in June of 1992. He was one hundred years old and was laid to rest in Dalat Cemetery in Vietnam.

In memory of my grandfather on my father's side, who died in April of 2000. He was eighty-three years old, and his ashes were scattered at his hometown in Hanover, Pennsylvania.

I could never have gotten through this process of writing without the support and encouragement of my beloved husband, Tasweer Memon, and my father, Jordan Wentz.

A special thanks to my uncle, Bernard Wentz, for letting me interview him about his experiences in the Vietnam War as a Marine.

Dr. Kraig Sturtz and Dr. Cindy Sturtz, for being true friends who believed in me. I never could have completed this memoir if they had not told their friends about my life experiences in Vietnam.

I won't forget my friend Dr. Sharon Bloom, who was very fascinated to learn about the lives of Amerasians. We met at Bataan Camp in the Philippines in 1989. We met again in 1994 in Philadelphia in the USA.

Dr. Khanh Che, for giving me the encouragement I needed.

Master Si Fu Qader A. Noorzad, for guiding me spiritually and to be self-reliant.

My best friend, Phat B. Duong, for his enduring support and for believing in me.

In memory of Kiet Bui, my fellow Amerasian friend.

For my lost Amerasian friend Hai, my classmate in second grade with Teacher Phuoc, somewhere in the USA. We came to see you when we heard the news that your mother was murdered at Nha Trang Beach, Vietnam.

For my lost neighbor, somewhere in the USA, my black Amerasian friend, nicknamed "Cuden," who was raised by Mrs. Du at Hong Bang Street, Nha Trang, Vietnam, and whom I invited to a New Year's celebration at my mother's house.

I would like to write my life's journal as a book for my children and to let them understand what their mother endured during the Vietnam War and give them some insight into the family history. As I was writing my book, Ameena, my four-year-old daughter, gave me some time by playing Spyro, a PlayStation game. Noah, my two-year-old boy, kept me company by climbing on my back as I sat on the chair in front of the computer, writing. I love you both very much!

Special thanks to the American government, the American embassy, and those who helped Amerasians come to the USA.

Misplaced

by
Angelina Wentz Memon

Amidst the violence that was the war in Vietnam, I was raised an Amerasian whose life was destined for struggle. The American soldiers had no knowledge of the future and did not know whether they would live or die, so they tried to find a way in which their hearts could be preserved. However, those who survived were held back, leaving their families behind.

Eighteen years passed before I was finally reunited with my beloved father.

Coming into the world with innocent cries, little did these babies know how guilty they would feel. In a bloody war, there was neither promise nor compromise, only days of heartache that persisted even after the war's conclusion.

I was born in Vietnam in 1969, at Hong Bang Hospital in Nha Trang. My biological father was there to witness my mother giving birth to me.

Thinking back on one's life is never easy. After more than three decades, my father still remembers the day he met my mother.

In Vietnam one particular evening when the base was quiet, a couple of my father's friends in his unit took him into Nha Trang city just to have a good time. My father wasn't a smoker or drinker, so he went off by himself.

Shortly after leaving his friends, he found an attractive young woman. He was looking for companionship, not just a one-night stand. They got along well, even though they had a language barrier. He was even accepted by her parents.

As a soldier, my father didn't have many chances to leave the base, so he tried to see her every chance he could get.

Three months later, my mother was pregnant with me. Both of them were overjoyed at the good news. Then the reality began to set in. They didn't know what the future would hold. My mother became tearful. She was hoping my father would stay longer in Vietnam. My father had told her she was his first love and the love of his life.

My grandmother packed clothes for my father and brought them to the hospital. He was excited and could not believe he had become a father at the age of twenty-one. We bonded with each other in a very short time. Three days after my birth, my father had to leave Vietnam because the Army ordered him to return home. It was the most difficult time for my mother, who cried for a long time after my father left for the United States. One month later, my mother gave me to my grandmother in Da Lat. My father had given my mother some money and furniture. She started working at a wood company to earn a living and sent milk and baby supplies to my grandparents every six months.

Every now and then, I think about Da Lat and the happy memories of my life with my grandparents. I felt very warm, safe, and happy when I was there, where I learned how to walk with my first baby steps and learned how to write the alphabet. I remember the first day of school; I held my grandfather's hand tight and wouldn't let it go in that strange place. We lived very close to the charming Lake Xuan Huong. The weather was cold and misty all year long. It was a lovely and romantic setting, especially when the leaves changed color and twisted in the wind. I picked tulips, daffodils, and dandelions. I loved to make necklaces from the flowers and wear them. I used to run merrily among the flowers, chasing the butterflies in my grandparents' garden, where they planted all kinds of vegetables—carrots, potatoes, and cabbage—on top of the hill next to the lake. In those lovely times, my grandmother sang lullabies, and the sounds of those sweet melodies will live with me forever. Then, one day, everything changed forever.

I will remember 1975 as long as I live and will never be free of the pain of my experiences during the war. One early morning, my mother came suddenly to my grandparents' house. After my mother and grandmother spoke briefly with each other, my grandparents cried and hugged me as they said good-bye. My mother and I left Da Lat and headed to Nha Trang, which was four hours away by car. We ran to the market to get some boxes of noodles and condensed milk. In the street, people panicked. They ran around screaming that the VC, the Communists, were coming. I had no idea what was going on. I watched as my mother packed hurriedly. She seemed to be lost and kept dropping suitcases on the floor. We waited patiently for a ride. Suddenly, outside the door, there were noises here and there of gunfire. My mother began shaking like a leaf, and I did not know how to help her. The sounds of gunshots became more aggressive. Everyone started locking doors. Luckily, Sergeant Tuc, my mother's neighbor, honked the car horn, and my mother and I ran to the car. We went to Cam Ranh Bay and took a boat to Saigon. We got into the large boat with much difficulty. People pushed each other to try to get in.

Some people did not know how to swim, and they drowned. Children lost their loved ones. The screams of children so traumatized me that I knew something wrong was going to happen. Then, the heavy rain started to fall. The raindrops hit my face like rocks. The boat headed out to the ocean, and the wind started to get stronger. The boat was overloaded and rolled heavily. We were soaked, like wet rats. The boat was moving slowly. People still followed behind. I heard a woman call out for her son. By that evening, everyone was exhausted. One man started to give out bread. People grabbed food from other people's hands. All of the bread dropped to the floor of the boat. The smell of people and the smell of old bread made everyone seasick. We headed to Saigon the next day. Sergeant Tuc left Vietnam for the United States a couple of days later.

From listening to the radio and hearing people's conversations, we realized Saigon would very soon fall to the Communists. People panicked and worried because they had no idea what was going to happen with their lives. No one knows what scared is until there is no peace. War isn't a joke.

We rented an apartment close to a place called Palace Doc Lap. I understood a little bit more about the war. My mother gave me a good shower and changed me into new clothes. That was the best memory about my mother. At night, I missed my grandmother dearly. The next morning, we headed out to the market for breakfast. We got some hoagie sandwiches and orange sodas. Suddenly, a group of people ran their motorcycles through the crowd. They stole food and trashed the place. Then, everyone ran in all directions, and people were running over each other. Some people got shot; others kept running. No one bothered to look back.

That night, everything was shut down early. The Saigon city was in peril. At midnight, I heard a gunshot very close by. I looked down the street and witnessed a horrible scene. I saw half of a burned hand falling from the sky onto the middle of the street. Even now, I wonder where that hand came from. My mother took me away from the balcony. We hid underneath the second-floor stairs. The gunshots became more aggressive. Exploding bombs were rumbling the city. The fire in the sky was nonstop. The landlord, who was the owner of a restaurant, was so scared from the explosions, he dropped to the floor. He wrapped himself with all of the pots and pans. I could not stop laughing each time he fell to the floor when he heard the explosions. The noise of pots and pans still reminds me a little of the humor in that scary time.

My mother and I were waiting for her boyfriend to pick up a suitcase at my mother's house in Nha Trang. It had all of the documents, such as birth certificates and bank paperwork; we needed to go to America. Finally, my mother's boyfriend came with bad news. He could not get the suitcase because my Aunt Ngan had refused to give a stranger my mother's personal things. Aunt Ngan had come from Pleiku with her husband and four children. She had been severely injured in an explosion, and the left side of her face was burned. My mother was so upset she had lost her money in the bank. The idea of going to America was crushed.

I was so happy for those who made it to the United States. I was so sad for those who lost their lives to find freedom. I was thrilled when I found out that a plane filled with mostly Amerasian orphans had taken off and had cleared the Viet Cong area with out getting shot down. The babies were going to their fathers' land--to freedom.

—◆—

On April 30, 1975, Saigon fell to the Communists. My mother and I rented another house close to the market. We went to the old house to pick up some of our belongings. We saw the second floor was badly damaged. Many bullets had gone through the walls and destroyed the balcony where I had slept the other night. My mother and I met two of my aunts, Aunt Du and Aunt Lien, and Cousin Tuyet at the supermarket. We were so happy together and planned to get back to Nha Trang.

A couple of weeks later, we all went back to Nha Trang. Everything happened so quickly, like a nightmare. The adults had their own worries, and the children had theirs. We all faced a difficult life ahead of us.

We walked into the house and said hello to my aunt's family. (They were living temporarily at my mother's house.) After some conversation, my mother had an argument with her sister about the suitcase she had refused to give to my mother's boyfriend and the jewelry that was missing. I was grateful to my aunt's family for saving our home. Unlike other neighbors' houses that were completely robbed by looters, we still had all of the valuables in the house. My aunt's face healed, but she had a scar from the explosion. My Aunt Ngan left the same day we got there and returned home to Pleiku. My mother and I spent a couple of weeks of quality time together. We learned how to bond with each other. I remembered our first dinner together. She made barbecue chicken marinated with lemongrass. She gave me my favorite drink, orange soda. I really enjoyed my mother's company.

The house itself, which consisted of three rooms, was nicely decorated. The guestroom was very nicely done. The ceiling's corners were hung with marble lights shaped like eggplants. A framed painting of deer in the forest hung above the door. All of the furniture was made of mahogany and stood out against the marble floor. My mother's room looked like the most expensive in the house. She had a queen bed sheet with a hand-designed picture of lovebirds on roses.

The closet door was of thick glass. It contained clothes and shoes from one end to the other. The look on my mother's face was priceless. She said happily, "Sweet home, my sweet home." That night, she hugged me to sleep.

My mother tried to hide me from the Communist soldiers. She told me not to come near them. She said they might kill me, and I should always be aware of my surroundings. Then one day, my mother's boyfriend appeared on our front step. My life changed from there. He got into the house uninvited by my mother. She did not agree with his coming there. He begged my mother to let him stay for a short period of time. He claimed he had nowhere to go. Soon, one day became a week, and weeks became months. He refused to leave, even through my mother confronted him many times.

The new government took over the entire country. Everybody was very frustrated that in so short a period of time, they went though such a major change. People still were unable to recover emotionally from the bloody war. They appeared more anxious. They had no idea what the future would hold. The change in people's lives was tremendous. They had to follow the new rules of the Communists. People had to register with the community center. They had to report their status and their family members. Those who had high status in the old government were taken to prison. Once again, people had to deal with unexpected separation. Thousands and thousands of people were locked up and transferred to a secret prison. They left behind their wives and children without any promise for the future.

My mother registered and included the name of my stepfather (her former boyfriend) on the family list. Every night, they went to a community meeting to learn how to be Communist citizens.

Despite all that happened, I remained an innocent girl wanting to play happily outside. Then one day, I went out with one girl from my neighborhood. We went to the Nha Trang City Beach. The beauty of the ocean fascinated me. I stepped on the white sand and wandered around the funny waves. I stared at the blue ocean, and suddenly, a strong wave took one of my slippers from my foot. After that, we chased each other around with a lot of excitement. Then we ran to a higher place. The surrounding area was covered with lots of sandbags. It used to be called the battle ditch, Dai Ham Nghi, meaning "the center to memory." The battle ditch was rectangular in shape. It was destroyed by the Communists a couple of years later. They used explosives to destroy the battle ditch. After that, it was a smooth sandy beach. That place reminded me that lots of soldiers had sacrificed their lives for the country, and they became forgotten. I jumped on top of the sand around the battle ditch. I was surprised to see a hand sticking out of the sand. I was scared and kept what I had seen a secret.

That evening, when I got home, my entire body was covered with red dots. The following day, I got a severe itch all over my body. The red dots started to open and spread extensively. My grandmother gave me a steam bath. She cooked herb leaves in a pot and covered my naked body with a blanket. The hot steam from the boiling herb leaves made me soaking wet. She cleaned my wound with a betel-nut-and-tobacco concoction, mixed with white wine. It prevented the itch for a short period. Shortly after that, the wound got infected, and white pus appeared. My grandmother did everything for me, but nothing seemed to work. At night, she comforted me by singing me songs. Those familiar songs reminded me of when I was a little baby. My mother was hopeless about my condition. She tried to give me western medicine. She gave me more penicillin and injected me with ampicillin. The medicine worked on the wound, and it became dry, but because of the dry skin, it caused more itching. My grandmother wrapped a thick cloth of cotton around my body. I went to school with long pants and a long T-shirt all year long so no one could see the wounds. I completed second and third grades.

━ ━

In the summer of 1977, my mother and my stepfather decided to send me to the Leprosy Hospital. The doctor ran some blood tests on me and gave me an examination. The doctor stuck a thick needle in my thigh, and I screamed from the excruciating pain. The test was to see if the patient experienced no pain from the needle. If so, that might indicate leprosy. The doctor reported a negative result for me. I learned so much on that day from observing the patients in the clinic. Patients with leprosy took baths with candle wax. I also witnessed people with fingers and toes missing; all of the fingers would soon fall off. Those who were in a more serious condition were admitted to the secret camp, deep in the mountain. Leprosy patients experienced pain when they faced the moonlight. People enjoyed the beauty of nature when the beautiful moonlight appeared. But leprosy patients had to run and hide from the moonlight. They had a song about the moonlight: "Who wants to buy the moonlight. I will sell the moonlight to you."

One day, my youngest aunt, Aunt Lien, came to us with wonderful news. She had just found one of the famous herb medicine monks. He lived outside the city in the suburbs. He examined me and gave me herb medicine. It tasted extremely bitter, and I had to be patient to drink it. At first, I vomited each time I drank it. Then, slowly, the medicine affected my system. The itch stopped, and the wound became dry. It all disappeared and left no scars. It took a long time for me to be a healthy girl again.

In 1978, my grandmother passed away. It was the first time I felt the kind of pain in my heart like a sharp needle sticking me over and over again. The pain was impossible to bear, and it never went away. It was the first time I learned how to cry with a broken heart. She got sick from a worm in her stomach. My mother and my aunts sent her to the hospital, where she was admitted to a critical care unit. She was given blood every other day. The disease was aggressive, and it sucked all of the blood that was given to her. She had an incurable disease. The doctor gave up and sent her home. She stopped breathing the next morning. I insisted my mother take me along to my aunt's house, but she refused to take me. I got there ten minutes late and missed seeing her for the last time. My mother tried to give her condensed milk at the last minute. She bit her lip because she could not touch the cow's milk. We all sat around my grandmother's bed to be with her for the last time on this earth.

At noon, I helped my grandfather to set up the table to pay respect to my grandmother. We placed her picture on top of the red cloth table. We put candles, incense, and flowers around it. My grandfather wrote old Chinese poetry to remember her legacy with a sweet and bittersweet memory. He was sobbing about her death. We invited two monks to come to pray all night long. We all stayed in front of her coffin to pray. At 2:00 p.m. the next day, when the funeral car stopped in front, my Aunt Du broke the plate to let her spirit go. Everyone screamed my grandmother's name. My mother did not go to the cemetery because of her pregnancy. We buried my grandmother on September 3, 1978, at Dong De Cemetery in Nha Trang.

I did not sleep for many nights after my grandmother died. I felt I had been tossed around in an open sea by strange waves. I became extremely sensitive, even to matters simple and sentimental. When I came home from school, I locked myself in the room for hours. I pressed her picture close to my heart and left it there. I started to write poems to express my sadness. I started to listen to the music because the world of music had brought relief to me when I was unhappy. It was a beautiful day, but the world seemed so empty.

The school helped me improve my knowledge. At the same time, I was free from many annoyances. During art period, Teacher Dung had us do a drawing of a coffin. I felt awkward, but I did my best, dedicating it to my grandmother. Ten days after my grandmother's death, my mother gave birth to a beautiful baby girl.

— —

In the New Year season of 1979, everybody celebrated another year to come with his or her loved ones. I invited two of my neighborhood friends to my house to celebrate. I offered a plate of sweet ginger and coconut and an orange soda. While we were eating, we watched a cartoon program about monkeys riding bicycles. We all laughed so hard. Suddenly, my mother got home; she screamed at me about how I dared invite those kids. One of them was an Amerasian black boy, Cuden, and the other was a mentally retarded girl, Hoa. She claimed those unfortunate kids would bring bad luck to our home for the entire year. I said I was sorry and asked them to leave. Surprisingly, she later said that year was the best year for her in her business.

In sixth grade, I had a wonderful teacher. She taught the literature class and was my ideal teacher. One day, she gave us a topic: "Describe the beauty of Nha Trang City's ocean, which you are living next to."

I began to write:

Here, the sunrise already came into the city. Here and far, the funny waves tried to jump on top of each other. There are many groups of boys and girls who come here to throw themselves into the sea waves and to breathe the fresh air of the sea.

I was so surprised that my paper was selected as a well-written example for the school. Teacher Chi was so proud to have me in the class.

Shortly after, my classmates started to hate me. They started to make fun of me and called me names such as "half-breed." The half-breed had twelve assholes, they sneered. I started to cry. Some girls collected lice from their hair and secretly put them on my hair. After class, as I started to head home, a group of girls pushed me back and forth. They laughed at me; their laughing chased me out of the school. One girl followed me outside to the street and jumped on me. She pulled my hair and kept punching me. I punched her back in order to get her to release my hair. One of my stronger punches left her with a swollen eye. She automatically let her hands go. My hair fell on the pavement. People watched us like we were crazy lions, but no one wanted to be involved in breaking up the fight.

The next school day, one boy in class kept hitting me. He slapped me so hard that I was afraid to go to school. I was afraid to let the authorities know. I was especially scared to tell my parents, because they would have hit me more no matter what. Every night, I prayed to God to let that boy stop hitting me. The abuse took place for a couple of weeks. One particular day, the boy kicked me hard in my stomach. That was it! I gathered all of my strength to hit back. I grabbed the boy and threw him into the corner of the blackboard. He was humiliated in front of all of the girls as they watched us. He left me alone after that incident. The school was getting a little bit easier for me. I didn't let those kids disrupt my education. I had to defend myself when I had to.

A couple of days later, in the middle of math class, someone came to look for the boy. He got excused from the class. He stormed out without his slippers. When school was dismissed, I brought the slippers to his house. I learned that his mother had just passed away. It was the last time I saw him. He didn't come to school anymore. He had to work to support himself. I felt really sorry for him.

The school was a safe place for me. My mother went on business trips from Nha Trang to Ban Me Thuoc. She was a very hardworking woman, who provided us with food and clothing. She came back home every two days. She bought coffee and tobacco, which were considered illegal items by the Communists, and wrapped the goods around her knees and under her belly with saggy bags with rubber bands. When she removed the bags, her skin had lots of red marks. She mixed the coffee seed with beans or corns to disguise the illegal products. The government prohibited these trading activities. The police squad arrested anyone doing it, and they lost everything. Sometimes, my mother lost all of her goods. At home, I took care of my half-sister so my mother had a peace of mind on her trips.

My neighbor, Miss Lat, was a fifth-grade teacher in my elementary school. She helped me with schoolwork and was there for me. She wrote a poem and read it to me, and I still remember it clearly:

> *Once I dreamed to be a teacher*
> *I would teach my pupils to be polite of*
> *Vietnamese tradition*
> *I would teach them all the famous poetic idioms*
> *From the beginning of our forefather's tradition*
> *'Cause our father of Vietnam's land was individual*
> *wise and hero.*

In the summer of 1980, my second half-sister was born. I was excited to have siblings, and I immediately became protective of them. I loved both of my half-sisters. I sang for them most of the time. I gently scratched their backs to put them to sleep. Outside, the hot wind of summer would burn every subject.

—◆—

In 1981, my childhood passed quickly. My imagination reminded me of my childhood. I was creating a private world for myself because of the children's innocent souls. The children's innocent world had encouraged me to pursue my ideal life to the end.

After hearing about a program for Amerasian children and their families to go to America, my mother decided to sell the house before we applied to go to the United States. If we did not sell the house, by law the government would seize it. We sold more than half of the house. We kept the last room and built an extra second floor on top of it. We had no well or public water in the house. We had to share the small fire lane temporarily. One day, when I dusted the furniture, I found five bars of twenty-four-karat gold, which belonged to the front house that was sold. I kept it in a secret place and gave it to my mother when she got home.

—◆—

The people who lived in the back of our home gave us problems. They figured we were soon to leave the country. They asked to be paid to let us use the small road that led to our house. My mother didn't agree, and they gave us two weeks' notice. My mother didn't take the notice seriously. Then, two weeks ended, and the owner of that house locked the door. We were stuck in the house the whole day. My mother became insane. She got a gasoline bottle and attempted to burn the house down. I begged her to be calm and to rethink her decision. I climbed down from the second floor using a long pole and ran to my neighbor to ask for help. Mrs. Le was a friend of my mother. I used a shovel to break the door. The door was made of hard steel, so I had to bend it all of the way. Mrs. Le and I entered the house. My mother was still holding the gasoline can in her hand. Upstairs, two of my half-sisters were crying aggressively. My mother didn't want to be bothered. Mrs. Le talked my mother out of the crazy attempt. She said, "You would go to jail if you burned the house down. Do you know that? Your children need you. Is it worth it to fight with those people? If you want to fight with them, you should go to the court." Thanks to Mrs. Le, my mother came to her senses. Upstairs, I gave condensed milk to my half-sisters. They were about to fall to sleep.

Then, outside the door, the owner of the back house was screaming about who had destroyed her door. I said I did it. I said we were locked inside the house without food and had no choice. Behind her, one of her sons called me "half-breed" and said I was the one who did it. I was extremely angry at the name-calling. I told him, "You'd better shut up." When I turned the other way, he beat me on my back with a very big stick. I grabbed his hands and finally got the stick from him. I kept hitting him, nonstop. His mother tried to rip my clothes, but I pushed her down to the cement floor. My mother was hiding inside the house behind the iron-barred window because she had just had plastic surgery on her nose. My mother used a broom to hit the boy to distract him. Then, someone called the police, and the police officer ordered the two families to meet at Police Station No. 7.

The police ordered the owner of the back house to unlock the door and wait for the court term. Every day, I had to carry water from the well one block away from our house. This was one of my chores. I thought my mother could have rented another small house that would have been more convenient. She was stubborn and had a hard time dealing with people.

A couple of months later, the small-claims court summoned my mother, and she lost the case. The owner in the back locked the door on us again. There was only one alley for a fire escape, and the alley belonged to all of the owners who lived there, which included my family, the house in back of us, and the house beside ours. My mother didn't settle on the court's decision. She asked the owner of the house beside ours to help her. They broke down one wall so we could get though. After that, they let us build a wooden bridge on top of their roof so we could go down. When we finished building the bridge, we built the cement wall back up to protect each other's privacy. My mother took a trip to Hanoi to send a letter to the Supreme Court, the top court in Vietnam. More than two years later, we got news from the Supreme Court that we won the case. I was so happy I didn't have to carry water to the second floor.

My mother registered me to attend private English classes. My teacher, Mr. Trac, was a very wise man, full of energy. He had a large forehead; which conveyed to me a rather high degree of intelligence. He kept his mustache shaped curly and had a habit of constantly touching the ends of it with his fingers.

He always dressed in a suit and loved having a cup of Ginseng tea while reading a magazine or a newspaper to keep him informed of the latest news of the day. He taught in seven languages; Russian, Japanese, French, English, German, Vietnamese, and Chinese. The class was called the International Class. I started with vocabulary, short sentences, and grammar. Mr. Trac taught me how to translate short essays from Vietnamese into English. I was so shy. I didn't speak English in the class, but I loved to translate all of the homework from Vietnamese to English on the blackboard. I had felt a promising horizon open widely to welcome me. My teacher's devotion was impressed upon my mind. I think he was a noble present the Creator had offered me to compensate for my unlucky fate. He was a man society could not slight because of his nobility. I still remember the question he asked while he was correcting my translation. "Will you remember me when you go overseas?" His question upset the equipoise of my sensitive nature. So I answered his question with silence.

—◆◆—

The school year was nearly over. My classmates decided to get together to go on a trip. We headed to the Ha Ra Bridge and to the Cau Bong River. Many people were going and coming over the bridge. To the right of the riverbank was a pagoda, Thap Ba. This place was built by careful and skillful architects. Many fishing villages were along the seaside with fishermen who devoted themselves to the sea waves day after day. Nha Trang is quite beautiful, poetic, and meek. That summer, I took a makeup exam for math class. I prepared for the ninth grade.

One day, someone told my mother he saw me with an old man around thirty years old and we were riding a motorcycle.

My mother was angry with me when she heard that. She asked me, "Anh, who was he?"

I answered, "I have no idea what he is talking about." I

told my mother I went over to my girlfriend Hang's house.

As my mother was worried that I may have slept with this "old man," she took me to the women's clinic. Dr. Luon was a well-known private doctor in Nha Trang. I saw pregnant women, who were about to give birth. They were crying and moaning outside of the room. I was very anxious about the surroundings.

Then, the door opened. Dr. Luon ordered me to get inside the room. I was told to take off my clothes. I was so embarrassed to do that. I held my pants tight and refused. The doctor insisted I should let her check me a little bit. "I have to take care of my patients outside who are waiting for me," she said. Her voice calmed me; I undressed and lay down on top of the steel table. She took a look with a bright light in my private parts. She was gentle in testing to make sure I was still a virgin. My mother stood next to us. Dr. Luon told my mother, "Your daughter is fine. No scar damage, and no sign of ripped tissue in her vagina."

My mother was relieved. I could have died from humiliation. I was so worried the other kids would find out, and if they saw me here, they would get the wrong impression about me. I would have rather died.

After that checkup, I was so nervous about associating with males. I showed no interest in being around people. I isolated myself as much as possible.

—◆—

In 1975, my mother had lots of nice clothes left over from the past. She fixed the clothes to my dress size and dressed me in them.

Sometimes, whenever I had some free time, I helped my Amerasian friend Van in my neighborhood by helping her sell banana rice cake, corn, and sweet potatoes. Van lived with her adoptive grandmother. They took good care of each other, in good times and bad times. Van finished sixth grade. She learned how to read and write despite the hardships of her life. The teasing of kids in the school and the violent behavior by a group of Vietnamese students caused Van to drop out of school. She didn't know her biological mother. She was told she had been sold by her mother when she was an infant. She was blessed to have a good foster parent, but she chose to stay with her foster grandmother. She came to the USA with her foster parent through the United Nations' Orderly Departure Program (ODP).

When I was talking with my Amerasian friends, I felt related to them. We all had a very similar situation. We all experienced the abuses, being abandoned and unwanted. We Amerasians were being tested constantly in the laboratory of life. We all came out stronger than ever. Will we ever truly have freedom of expression about who we are? We were always feeling we were cheated and robbed, not only of our rights and honors, but also of the very means of existence and companionship every person deserves. Living in a discordant and cruel world, we have gathered our will to struggle against ourselves when we felt discouraged. We are what we are, unchangeable, regardless of whether our childhood was trapped in terrible circumstances.

We Amerasians were the result of a beautiful thing that happened in a bloody war. We were born into the world and took our first breath; our cry could be the most beautiful sound that could heal the world. We were a most beautiful gift to mankind, which God created. We have to recognize our purpose in order to be stronger in life. Although our faith is shaken, we must believe that things don't just happen, but that everything is part of a great plan. We are a reason why American and

Vietnamese were connected because we hold the blood of both within. We all have had both places to call home. We got a mixed look and intelligence and more common sense in life in order to survive. Our fathers are American heroes: soldiers who died, those still alive or unknown. We are sons and daughters of those soldiers. We are grateful to have Vietnamese mothers who gave us lives. We Amerasians have got to stop playing victims because nobody cares unless we do. We all need love; love comes no matter what the circumstances. We need motivation to help each other to do well. When we are feeling better and improve our self-image and sense of mastery, together we can do it!

❧—❧

One of my Amerasian friends was a most beautiful girl. Her face had a delicate look, like a movie star. Wherever she went, people turned their heads to admire her beauty. She lived just a few blocks away from my house. This girl was molested by her alcoholic stepfather when she was in fourth grade. She left the house and hooked up with a businesswoman who was involved in transporting illegal items, such as coffee and tobacco. Because of her beauty, she got away from the Communist policemen while they were looking for the illegal goods. She was good at pickpocketing the Communist soldiers if they flirted with her. When the train stopped, she would give back all of the items to the owner. In return, they gave her some money for doing her part.

She had a great relationship with her real mother, who was stuck with an alcoholic husband and five kids. Her mother worked very hard to support them by selling shrimp rice cakes at the market. Each time my friend came home for a visit, her mother welcomed her with open arms. At sixteen years of age, this girl got married to a Chinese man who owned the house supply store at the Saigon market. She was abused by her husband and ran away with her infant son. She and her mother secretly applied to the Orderly Departure Program. She registered her mother and five of her siblings.

One of my other friends had golden fair hair and a baby face. She looked a lot more American than Vietnamese. She had been found in the trash can in front of the gold store. The owners found her when she was a couple of months old. They raised her along with their own children. She had a chance to pursue her education and seemed very happy with her adoptive parents. I got a chance to meet her and her adoptive parents' family in Bangkok, Thailand, where we all waited for the paperwork, so that we could continue the trip to America

—▬ ▬—

In 1982, I was in my last year in elementary school. I made more friends. School was less violent for me, but instead of dealing with bullying kids, I now faced discrimination. I realized that I had to work extra hard to finish my education. The tension between the Communist students and me was very high whenever I got a good grade on a topic about politics of the VC, the head of government, and Uncle Ho Chi Minh. One of my classmates was furious with me when I got an excellent grade on an essay. She ripped my paper away from my hand. She said with tears, "You are an Amerasian. You should know less about Communists, and I am a daughter of Communists, I know better than you."

She was right. I was just a writer. I had learned from Ho Chi Minh's theory that "Nothing is of more value than living in a society with independence, freedom, and happiness." And "Rich folks need to share their material with the poor folks."

Unfortunately, the Communists of the government of Vietnam were despotic and cruel. They suppressed intellectuals. They didn't obey their Uncle Ho. They were really abusing his wishes. They robbed their citizens of life. The whole country fell into poverty and had no way to turn. People had no choice but to escape to a different country. People died from hunger. Depression led them to commit suicide. People died from the torture of hard labor in the deep jungle or lost their lives in storms at sea. Vietnam, the beautiful countryside, seemed a haunting place.

That year was a study year for all of students in ninth grade who would enter high school. After the regular exams at the end of the year, the students in ninth grade had to take one more major exam in math, literature, biology, and chemistry. The high school limited the number of new students who could enroll. So they were very strict in grading the papers. Only fifty percent of the students who got accepted entered the two main high schools in Nha Trang; Ly Tu Trong High School and Nguyen Van Troi High School.

My mother gave me a party to celebrate my moving up to the Ly Tu Trong High School. She proudly invited one of the neighbors, who worked in the government courthouse. I was a friend of his daughter. We had spent many times studying together. At the end of the school year, her father didn't want me to study with his daughter. He told me to let his daughter study alone. He would lie to me to avoid me having any contact with his daughter. He was positive his daughter had more knowledge to pass the exam than I. He had high status in the Communist government. The school gave two extra points to his daughter in order for her to pass the exam. Unfortunately, she still could not make it to the main high school. She attended a different high school in the city.

My mother gave me a necklace as a gift. I really appreciated the party my mother had given me. I was grateful for her confidence in me. That night, I looked at the moonlight spread all over my neighborhood. Everything seemed still, and I started to write the poems "A Moon Light in the Summer Night" and "Sea Lover."

At the beginning of the high school year, I was assigned to 10 A-3. All of the students practiced how to operate guns made of wood sticks. We were marching like in an army. We gained some knowledge about how to be soldiers. Then, we learned how to dance with a partner in class. I was voted to be a leader of singers in my class. I had to learn a new song before the class started. I taught them how to sing a new song in every first period of class.

At school, we had to study Russian for a second language. We had to memorize all of the lessons and demonstrate in front of class. I signed up for the marathon event in the school. I won first place on the girls' team. I received a dozen notebooks, pens and pencils.

On a class trip, we got a chance to greet Prime Minister Pham Van Dong at Nha Trang Airport. The students were excited to greet him with flowers and songs, but I felt somewhat awkward and misplaced to see a Communist leader. When the prime minister got off of the plane, the students pushed each other to get closer. I was standing still, and then I had the weirdest feeling. I wondered if I belonged there. It was sort of like a weird dream that happened in my awake life.

—◆—

My mother quit making the business trips from Nha Trang to Ban Me Thuoc. A group of people lived in the jungle called the Red Khmer stopped the cars and robbed people. Later, the Red Khmer shot up a bus that carried a lot of passengers. My mother's bus was few minutes behind. My mother witnessed the death of her girlfriend. She left a husband and five young children. The youngest one was only three months old. My mother and I went to their house to pay respects and helped them with some money for the funeral. That night, my mother came to realize she had just escaped from death.

My mother went to learn cosmetology at the local beauty shop. Mrs. Mai-Ly, the instructor, had learned cosmetology in Japan. My mother practiced hairstyling on me. She started to dress nicely that summer. I hadn't seen her like that in so many years. She had always worn black pants and a purple blouse. They were all torn and faded. She really needed a change.

— —

In October 1984, we finally got our passports. I prayed every night to God to please just take me to America as soon as possible. I wrote a letter to my father. I let him know I had received a passport.

A letter to my father!
I really love you! Do you remember me or did you forget me? However, I am still your daughter. Every night I prayed that one day I could see you. Best wishes to you and my grandparents. Daddy, why is my life so difficult without you, Father? Do you think that matters? I shall do good deeds, and I shall be a

virtuous girl, so you will be proud of your daughter. When I realize that, I commended myself to do my best for mankind during my lifetime. (...) No one could imagine that people could fly, but I want to fly to you, Father. My impression about you is that I look like you. What is the shortest way from Nha Trang to Pennsylvania? How far is the earth, can I tell you? My family and I have had the passports since October of 1984. So, I hope I will see you soon. Daddy, who does the shopping in the family? Who takes care of Grandfather? I will help you when I get there. I want to be a writer or artist when I grow up. I miss you, Daddy,
Love,
Your daughter!
Ngoc Anh

One month after I wrote that letter, I received a letter from my father along with his picture. My father also sent me a short poem:

Love is everything
Love needed a little rain to help it grow
Went through storm rain, heartache or pain
Real love is never change!

The years rapidly passed. I wondered what my father looked like and thought of how I missed him, even though I was living with my imagination.

It was a miracle to hold my father's picture in my hands. How sad it was after I saw his photo. I wished I could kiss his fair hair, the hair that had gone through the ups and downs of life, and kiss his deep eyes, the eyes that had been waiting for his daughter, who was separated by the Pacific Ocean. The gloomy air enclosed me. Why does time fly slowly?

In 1985, my family went to Saigon for our appointment
with the American interviewers. We stayed at the home of
my stepfather's sister in the town of Binh Trieu. We took
a trip to visit all of the pagodas around the city. Saigon was
crowded and fast living. At night, from the harbor, Saigon
looked like a pearl of the East. The city was full of people,
cars, taxi, buses, motorcycles, bicycles, tricycles, rushing
by each other, horns blaring. With the smell of gasoline
and the dust flying in the humid city, Saigon was on the
move.

The interview day finally arrived. At the emigrations
office gate, in the early morning, my family and a group of
Amerasian children and their families were all waiting for
a bus to take us to the main center.

I was thrilled about American sympathy toward
Amerasian children. Like angels, they came here to rescue
us. It was our life's best moment. My emotions left me
speechless. In years past, Amerasian children had lived in
a forsaken place, regarded as parasites of society. I had an
idea that Amerasians drifted to Vietnam from a far planet,
to a bad, wicked, dirty, and sinful marsh. We longed to be
rid of it. We were living in a sorrowful environment in
stuffy and mean air, which can defeat anyone who has not
the patience or brains to withstand it. The American
dreamland was the only way out for Amerasian dignity.
We longed for it, like weeds need fog to live. We loved it like
all of the creatures on this earth love their breath. It was
a star that lightened our souls during the most desolate
and tragic nights. We longed to go to our fatherland.

The interview went well. It was an emotional day for me. All of the Amerasian children who had the same life experience surrounded me. I had a chance to contact American people. They were also my people. Everything seemed so beautiful on that day--the sky, the people, and the lovely scenery. I was a dreamer!

Right after the interview, we went to the famous supermarket Ben Thanh, in Saigon. My mother treated us to a special meal. It was called Pho beef noodle soup. Then, we shopped for new clothes for our departure.

We returned to Nha Trang almost a month later.

I no longer went to the public high school. In eleventh grade, it helped me somewhat to get more knowledge to adjust. I was home studying the book of essays more. I memorized all of the short essays and poems, and I tried to help my classmates at Ly Tu Trong High School with their literature essays. My mother decided to let me attend a private English class full time. Every day, while I washed the clothes next to the well, I waited for the mailman to bring the letter from America. I had no desire to live in Vietnam any longer. My mind was set on an American dream. I wanted to go further with my education. Especially, I wanted to meet my father. Then things didn't work out the way our family had planned. We didn't get permission to leave the country because of court papers. My mother tried to keep the small house we were living in for the relatives. Our situation was so complicated. In order to leave the country, three essential documents were required: a signature from the Department of Real Estate, a debt-free statement from the Central Bank of Vietnam, and a certification from the Department of Taxation. My family didn't complete the signed documents from the Department of Real Estate that were required by the Vietnamese government. Things had gone well for those who had passports at the same time as us. They were all long gone to America. A couple of months later, the ODP program was delayed to evaluate the cases of Amerasians and their families who wanted to go to the USA. Once again, Amerasians were robbed of their rights. Some Vietnamese unrelated to Amerasians tried to get passports to the USA. They faked being married to Amerasians, threatening, cheating, and persuading Amerasians to claim them as relatives or husbands or wives. It was an outrage, unspeakable, and an injustice for Amerasians to be victimized.

My mother was shocked at the news. We had no idea when the ODP program would be rescheduled. I was doomed by the news. America seemed so far away; the space between us was the Pacific Ocean. Around me, everything seemed to stop to listen to the sound of my sighs.

Every day, when it was schooltime and when it was over, I looked out my window, where students passed through, to look for something in those innocent souls that was shown by their eyes. I missed my old school and my old friends. I remembered sadly that in the Vietnamese New Year, a group of students from my high school class all came to say Happy New Year to me. I hoped my classmates were still my friends.

I missed the interview with the Americans in Saigon. A ray of hope for my future just flashed in my mind. My application was approved, but there was nothing more restless than a promising departure. My nerves were weak. Then, I created a method to cure my nerves by managing to do good deeds such as fasting, being vegetarian, and helping the poor. I saved some of my breakfast money to give to the beggars.

One old lady who lived in my neighborhood was taking care of an unwanted baby that belonged to one of her nieces. The niece was in jail, charged with prostitution. Every day, the old lady carried the baby to the corner of the street to beg for money. The baby was constantly crying from poor nutrition and the burning heat of the hot summer day. The old lady did her best; sometimes, she didn't have enough money to buy condensed milk. She gave him water cooked from old rice instead. The neighbors hesitated to help because they believed the baby was born out of wedlock. At night, I gave the baby some of my half-sisters' leftover milk. The baby died a couple of months later from hunger and from yellow ant bites. All of the neighbors chipped in money for the funeral the next day. I prayed that the poor baby's soul would go to heaven.

The old lady became so weak. I washed her clothes when I finished washing my family's clothes. From sitting on the streets, her clothes were very dirty; they were soaked and wet with urine. I poured water on them, then soap, and stepped on them with my slippers.

One night, there were strange noises outside my house. A couple knocked on my door and asked for my name. I told them. They told me they were relatives of the old lady. Their voice had an accent that Chinese people had when speaking Vietnamese.

I asked them, "Do you speak the Chinese language?"

They both replied, "Yes. We speak fluently."

I walked with them to the old lady's house. They were dressed very well. The man wore a gray business suit. The lady wore a very expensive white silk outfit. She wore gold bangles and a necklace. Her hair was curly and was put up in a French style.

The night before, the old lady had almost passed away. The next-door neighbor went through all of the old papers in the old lady's house. She found one of the addresses, then she sent a telegram to Saigon. Finally, the old lady's relatives came and helped her to move to their house to take care of her. I gave the old lady a hug and she kept looking at me with thanks in her eyes. Then, when they were all about to leave, the old lady's relatives offered me a sum of money that was in her hand. I was shocked she would even think about giving me the money. I refused right away. I was so happy the old lady was in good hands. I ran home feeling good about my good deed. I was surprised my neighbor had recognized my work.

— —

We were running into some financial problems. My mother sold most of the gold we got from selling the front of the house. For almost two years, we didn't hear anything about the ODP program. My mother was under lots of stress because nobody brought any income into the household. My mother decided to go back on the business trips. She carried illegal tobacco from Saigon to Nha Trang. She did it once or twice a month. I asked my mother if I could go with her. I hid the whole box of cigarettes on my legs. My mother helped me wrap rubber bands around my legs to hold it. We stayed in the motel near the bus station in Saigon and took the cigarettes and sold them to the small shop. I experienced the hard work my mother had done for us so many years!

My stepfather worked on filling out the applications for those Amerasians and their families with a little money. He did the paperwork for those who got sponsored by their loved ones from overseas. When they got called for an interview, he took a trip to Saigon. It was a simple matter, but it was difficult for those who did not know how to read or write in the Vietnamese language. Most of his clients were from the fishing village. My stepfather charged them an expensive price: one or two 18-karat gold pieces. My stepfather earned some money for our family.

———

One late evening, after I'd had some argument with my step-father, I had no desire to stay with my family any longer. I didn't go to the private English class. I ran away from home! I was walking alone in the street, and I had no particular place to go. Suddenly, two of my friends in the private English class, Dong and Trang, saw me. They tried to ask me where I was going. I tried to explain, but no words came out from my mouth. They both insisted I go to their parents' home. When I got to their parents' house, I was so nervous at first, but after the warm welcome, I felt understood!

Dong was born with a birth defect. One of his legs was completely paralyzed. In the class, Dong was a very smart student, but he never attempted to go to the blackboard to do his homework. He was so shy and worried that the students would laugh at him. When the class was dismissed, he and his brother were the last ones to come out of the class.

I noticed Dong had some physical impairment. I decided to talk to him after the class. I told him he didn't need to hide from me. His younger brother was so happy that I did not look at his brother any less. Instead, I wanted to be their friend if they wanted me to. Trang was the bodyguard for his brother. He helped his brother through all of the high school years. They both wanted to be teachers.

I stayed at Dong and Trang parents' house for about a month. One of their younger sisters, Vang, was kind enough to share her room with me. I asked Dong and Trang to come to my cousin's house to get the information. Tuyet was a very close cousin of mine. We had gone to school together. We shared a lot of childhood memories. She knew what I had been through. Tuyet was the only child of my Aunt Du. My Aunt Du came to Dong and Trang's house to give me the good news. My flight finally was here! I said thanks and good-bye to their family. Dong broke down and cried hysterically. I felt so sad to say good-bye to my best friend. On the other hand, I felt overjoyed.

Aunt Du took me to my mother's house. My mother rushed me to pack for the trip to Saigon the following day. She warned me not to let anyone know about our trip. I was so worried about delay. That night, I sat in the corner of the room to pray. I left some my items for my cousin to have: clothes, books, and some old toys.

The next day, early morning, I ran to my aunt's house; I stood there and cried. I had a very difficult time saying good-bye to my grandfather. Since my grandmother had passed away, he had become closer to me. My cousin was my grandfather's favorite niece. I was my grandmother's favorite. In that moment, all of the happy times we shared together were rolling in my mind. My first day in school, I held my grandfather's hands and didn't let go in a strange place. He gave me a hug and kissed me softly on my forehead. He cried and told me to be a good citizen in a foreign land. He told me to take good care of myself by taking herb medicine. I had saved some money in my pocket to give to him as a small gift. I ran out the room with the words, "I love you, Grandfather." I couldn't bear to see him; I sobbed.

Time was running out. I ran so fast to my girlfriend's house. Hang was my very closest friend. We had met in sixth grade. She was my loyal friend. I was always grateful to have a friend like her. I saw her eyes fill with tears. I didn't want our friendship to be dimmed by being apart.

In a hurry, I ran home to get my bags. My family and I had to leave at 7:00 a.m from the bus station. A few minutes before the bus was about to leave, I saw Dong and Trang in the corner of the street. On the other side of the street was my best friend, Hang. They had all come to see me for the last time. I would have liked to run to them. I stood there with a broken heart. Then, the bus ran faster and faster. I looked behind and saw Hang wave good-bye. Dong and Trang chased our bus on their motorcycles. When the bus slowed down in the crowded street, they threw a pair of guavas to me. We all waved till the bus was lost in the crowded street.

At nightfall on July 1, 1988, the bus stopped at the Saigon bus station. We took a three-wheel motorcycle to my stepfather's sister's house. That night, after I finished giving dinner to my half-sisters, I rushed to my bag to make sure that some of the seashells in the box were okay. I received those gifts from Dong, Trang, and Hang. I put the box in a safe place. I didn't forget the diary book from my elementary school. I felt more relaxed, after all.

A week went by. My family had a problem with the Department of Real Estate. The small house my mother saved to give to her relatives didn't get approval. My mother sent my stepfather back to Nha Trang to resolve the problem right away. We were patiently waiting for his telegram so my mother could sign the house over to the government. Something went wrong with the paperwork, and our flight was canceled! The news hit my ears like thunder.

In Saigon, I had no letters or telegrams from my mother. My two half-sisters and I stayed at my stepfather's sister's house. There were ten people in the house. Every day, his sister gave me some money to prepare food for them. The meals were my idea. I cooked meals such as French tomato ground beef, fried fish with lemongrass, sweet-and-sour tomato soup, and chicken with ginger, fried crispy. They enjoyed every single meal I made. After the meal, I did all of the dishes and washed clothes for everyone. I mopped the floor every night by hand so we had a clean place to sleep. My mother gave them two big bags of rice and some money for us to stay.

I was overstressed. One day while I was cooking, I felt dizzy and passed out on the floor. The lady who lived next door gave me a coining on my back, arms, and neck, in the Vietnamese tradition of medicine. I felt much better after that! That night, I wrote a letter to all of my friends to let them know I was still stuck in Vietnam.

More than a month later, my mother and my stepfather arrived. I had no idea what was going on about the trip to the USA; I just did my chores.

Why was this happening to me? I thought, *I was born to bargain over my life with a long and troubled chain of endurance because of many results that are not created by me.* I became so anxious about my flight to the USA. I dreamed I had been a single traveler on an endless journey. Then there were God's hands, which led me to take part in my journey by chance. At least, no one could take my dream away!

—◦ ◦—

September 12, 1988, was an eventful day in my life. I had been waiting for this moment for so many years, through all of the heartache, depression, and desperation for a promising journey. I rushed myself through the passenger departure door, hoping I could catch this flight as fast as my heartbeat. It was my last attempt. I dropped myself on the bench with a ticket in my hand. Nervously, I listened for my family's names to be announced.

Next to me, both of my half-sisters chased each other with innocent laughs. My mother ran to the cafeteria to spend her last Vietnamese money on a soda. Behind me, my stepfather screamed happily toward his sister's family, his smile never fading. I was silently crying with overwhelming emotion. I looked at the blue sky with the clouds running until they disappeared on the distant horizon. The sun spread all of the diamond rays of the heat, creating all variations in color. A day I never dared to forget! The day I left Vietnam.

Suddenly, the door opened, the bell suddenly rang, and the passengers ran toward the main entrance. The security people checked passengers' suitcases like hungry wolves. They demanded money or items from passengers. If they did not get anything, they either cursed the passengers or pushed them away. The bad memory of this kind of treatment from the Communists caused people to leave the country even faster.

Outside, the noise of people shouting became louder and louder. Handkerchiefs waved in the sky. People kissed each other with their eyes. That was the last time I saw my aunt's figure slowly fading into the crowd.

The airplane was slowly moving on the runway. I took a deep breath, dreaming merrily about my journey.

Looking through the airplane's window, I saw the beautiful sky as the world settled over me like a soft blue blanket. Here and far, those clouds kept running toward me. When the teardrops weren't yet dry on my face, we landed at Bangkok's airport. There, we had to do more paperwork and have photographs taken. A couple of hours later, we all moved into a small camp to wait for another plane's departure for the Philippines.

Finally, at nightfall, I had a chance to engage with other Amerasian families. We said hello to each other and shared sad and happy stories. It was a great feeling! We felt the connection and acceptance of Amerasians around all of us. Tired after our journey, we all tried to get some sleep. I was so excited to meet new acquaintances, but I wouldn't forget the farewell of my friends in Vietnam. I opened the suitcase to get the gift from my best friends Hang, Dong, and Trang, but I discovered it was still in Vietnam. I broke out crying like a baby having its toy taken away, but then I dried my tears quickly.

The next day, Amerasians and family members were flown to the Philippines for another six months at the Philippine Refugee Processing Center. We learned English and were taught about American culture and work habits. My family and I were assigned to Cycle 124. We shared rooms with people who had escaped from Vietnam by boat. I heard some heartbreaking stories. Have you ever escaped from your country? No one could understand the impressions of the refugees when they truly leave their country.

Dung was truly the strongest survivor I ever knew. Dung, his brother, and his sister-in-law all escaped from Vietnam to Cambodia by boat with a group of people. At Kompongsom seaport in Cambodia, they got into a small motorboat, with a group of people in the boat. They headed to the sea, and twenty-four hours later, they ran into a big storm. The sky became darker and darker. The sea wind rose up suddenly and angrily. Waves rose up and down like primitive dinosaurs wanting to swallow their boat into the sea. Their boat was like a small leaf in the ocean. The water came into their boat, so they had to bail the water out every minute. Their boat jumped up and down from the wild waves. They were lost in the sea without any idea where they were. Then, the storm stopped after two consecutive days. Everyone felt hungry, tired, and thirsty. They didn't know where they could go to get to the mainland.

They were lost in the ocean for almost thirty days. People died slowly from lack of nutrients and water, fearful and hopeless. They fought with each other over food. The dead bodies were thrown into the deep ocean. The motor in their boat was broken. They felt disappointed but trusted in God and their boat. At that time, Dung couldn't cry anymore. He was scared, starving, and desperate to live. They ate wood from the boat, the slippers, and whatever they found on the boat. The hunger turned them into monsters. They were lying in the lost boat and hopelessly waiting for the miracle rescue. Dung, his brother, and his sister-in-law fought with each other. Dung got knocked out of the boat. Death was getting closer and closer. Dung had no energy to swim. Finally, his brother jumped down, and with a struggle, they got into the boat.

After almost thirty days lost in the ocean, they were saved by a fishing boat that took them to the Philippines. Ten people lost their lives in this journey. Dung got very sick from hemorrhoids He was hospitalized for a couple of months. Dung's brother and his wife were in poor condition. They lost a lot of weight; his brother's wife weighed only thirty kilograms. Some people survived, but they suffered tremendously from the loss of their loved ones in the ocean. They became angry and were fighting with each other constantly. I couldn't believe it when I heard this story from Dung. He kept this secret and suffered with guilt. Every night, he hid in the dark corner, holding the incense and praying for his soul. I comforted him by understanding how a human being learned how to survive in such circumstances. This was beyond his limits. His passion to look for a land of freedom was realistic. Dung was one of the Vietnamese who paid a very high price for his freedom. I hoped time would heal his pain and treat him kind. I thanked him for sharing his unbelievable story. I wished that Dung would see his story as more pitiful than blameworthy. He blamed himself for having a chance to live while his companions died. Dung, his brother, and sister-in-law moved to Australia in 1990. They were united with their uncle.

‑ ‑

While living in the Philippines for six months, I learned a great deal about English and about American culture and work habits, especially from a program in volunteer work. All of the refugees had to do volunteer work outside from 9:00 a.m to 11:00 a.m. We had to attend school from 1:00 p.m to 5:00 p.m. I did my volunteer work at the dental office. Also, I was an interpreter of English into Vietnamese for the patients. I was a dental assistant and felt useful to the community. I joined the youth activities club. I won a marathon in second place. I tried my best with lots of hard work and dedication. I set my goals and learned how to complete them.

My graduation marked the beginning and the end of many things. From what I learned in a short period, I would face life in the USA more or less prepared. My family and I were so excited to finish the English as a Second Language program. We received a list of people who were going to depart for America on May 9, 1989. I was excited that my family and I were on that list. Unluckily, I got malaria right after receiving the good news. I was admitted to the hospital for four days and had to take medicine and blood tests for a month. My list was canceled by the ICM (Inter-Governmental Committee on Migration) office. I was so disappointed and exhausted after all that. It seemed like I was carrying the entire weight of the world on my shoulders.

Every day, I spent most of my time dreaming of the day I'd be gone. My family and I waited patiently for almost a year. Then, one day Dung saw my name on the departure list at the local office. I ran to the office to see the list with my own eyes. My family hurried and packed on short notice, and we prepared a trip to the Manila Airport. When the bus started, Dung gave me fifty pesos, Philippine money, as a gift. I shall never forget him.

＿＿

We had finally landed at the Philadelphia airport and were waiting for our sponsor to pick us up. A group of Vietnamese people came for us. They were introduced to us as members of the Mennonite church. The pastor gave us a quick handshake. We got in the car to go home. We were moving down the busy street, and Philadelphia at night looked so beautiful. For me, it was a new trip, full of expectations of miracles and adventures, in the unknown country.

Our sponsor dropped us at an apartment in West Philadelphia. We had two bedrooms and mattresses on the floor for us to sleep on. They gave us a bag of old clothes. There was a refrigerator with a few items and twenty pounds of rice. That was it.

A couple of days later, they showed us the supermarket. They took us to the welfare office to fill out all of the paperwork. My family and I got a lot of help from Amerasians who had come before us. Kiet was an Amerasian friend who took my two half-sisters and me to the testing center. We all took the tests in math and English. Based on the scores on our exams, they placed us in the appropriate grade level. Both of my half-sisters were placed in elementary school. I had a high score in math and English, so they assigned me to twelfth grade in South Philadelphia High School. When I entered the high school, a teacher disagreed that twelfth grade was the appropriate grade level for me. She asked me to take another exam. I asked the principal to clear up the matter. Principal Jung asked me nicely to take another exam because he didn't want to upset his colleague. I got accepted into twelfth grade. I wrote an essay to enter the essay contest in school, and to my surprise, I placed first. Principal Jung had a picture taken with me at the awards dinner. That year, school lunch was canceled because of a fight that had occurred between students the previous year. After school, I went to work at a pizza place until closing at midnight.

At school, Teacher Kaik was very kind to me. She sent me to the school counselor to talk about everything that I had to cope with. My main goal was to work for my graduation and apply for admission to college.

Because I was a newcomer to the USA, some young guys from the Mennonite church came to my house and offered a television, tables, and some furniture. I refused because I felt nothing was free. Some boys were flirting with me, but I wasn't interested because I was daydreaming, imagining what my life was going to be. *I am more than my problem,* I knew.

Every Sunday, the people in the Mennonite church took us to the Sunday Bible School. I had a chance to meet new friends. I got to know Tuan, an Amerasian. He was a very friendly and sensitive person. From the first day when I came to the USA, he was always there to help my family. Tuan was a hard worker and helped anyone in need. He was a real picture of sincerity and truthfulness; anyone should have a friend like him. Tuan had a limited education because of his difficult life in Vietnam. He had very sharp common sense and patience. He was well aware of what I had been going through.

One Saturday night, my mother had a dinner for members of the Mennonite church. They came to our place to study the Bible and pray together. After that, we treated them with a special dinner. We made shrimp egg rolls and beef noodle soup and had a tea party. My Amerasian friends--Kiet, Ha, and Tuan--came, as well. We had a lovely time together. After everybody left, I helped my mother with the dishes.

I had always felt that my mother and my stepfather loved my half-sisters much more than me, and that night, I wrote a letter to my father. I asked him to see me soon. Then I gathered all of my energy to prepare for exams.

June 15, 1990, was my high school graduation day. We were practicing the songs. I was so thrilled with all of the excitement around me. Teacher Kaik came to the ceremony; we took a picture and wished each other good luck. My Amerasian friend, Tuan, drove me to the Civic Center for the graduation ceremony.

My father sent me a letter and a two-way ticket to his house. His truck was in the shop at the time. He lived three hours from Philadelphia. I was very scared of being lost going to the bus station, and the ticket expired, after all. I was so sad I couldn't see my father.

— —

June 24, 1990, was my day! My Amerasian friend Tuan drove me to my father's house. We left Philadelphia on a hot summer day. I could only sense the desire we shared about looking for an American father. The thought flashed into my brain and was gone before I even knew it had been there. The idea that I was going to my father's home—I was overjoyed! I wrapped these thoughts around my head as the car went faster down the road. For lunch, we had a bag of chips and soda. Tuan turned the music on. The song's words--"Waiting for you. Wherever you go, whatever you do, I will be right here waiting for you..."--played exactly into my emotions. The music brought tears to my eyes.

The closer I got, the further my thoughts went, and my walk got softer. I came to my father's hands. His eyes filled with tears. He kept repeating over and over, "It was such a long time to see you."

Like a baby, I lay on my father's shoulder. I could feel myself growing stronger, with someone to love that I barely knew I had, until I began to share it with my own father, the father that I lost in war, eighteen years ago. He held me in his arms just like when I was three days old. The father I dreamed of as a child really did exist. This moment will last with us for a lifetime. In the corner, I heard Tuan sobbing. He cried happy tears for me, sad that he did not know who his father was. My heart broke to see him that way. I held him, and the three of us hugged each other. I shared this special moment with the father I had just found with the Amerasian friend whose father was lost.

We dried the tears and took some pictures for remembrance. Tuan and I got ready to go back home the same day. It was an evening close to midnight without moonlight. I recollected it in my memory with special love and tenderness.

I felt less lonely. I had so many plans in my dream. It was just a beginning. I smiled.

A couple of months later, my father came to visit my mother and me. My mother was so overwhelmed to see her lover after eighteen years. The joy in their faces as they stared at each other was magical. They handled it in such a way that it became a gesture of love. They both looked vulnerable and glanced at me, the child they had. I left the room so they had some time to share their love. She learned one thing: my father was still single. Their conversation became a little awkward, like they had knots in their throats. They became shy and hesitant. I hadn't seen my mother so charming and lovely like that evening. She was the mother I used to remember in the past.

My stepfather walked into the house with a very heavy face. In ignorance, he passed by us without saying a word. My father said good-bye to us in a hurry. That evening, a glorious rainbow appeared over our house. The sun appeared as it retired for the day's end, sending streaks of beautiful red, orange, and yellow across the deep blue sky. From far away, the birds flew farther and farther and got lost in the distance. The night fell so quickly.

On July 12, 1993, I was at the Art Museum in Philadelphia, walking with my boyfriend. We had walked from the community college to the park after class was dismissed. The park was crowded with people and tourists. The trees, the flowers, and the grass were full of life. The birds sang, and the flowers perfumed the air with nature's scents. The statues created a historical scene.

I called my half-sister and received the news that Kiet, my Amerasian friend, had been shot by an Italian motorcycle gang in South Philadelphia. I screamed and was in shock. I ran home right away to go to the funeral home. He was shot seven times in his chest and head. He took the bullets for his friends in the car. The drive-by shooting was never investigated. They couldn't identify the murderer.

It was outrageous that his death went unnoticed. No word to describe the loss of a child. His mother mourned and begged God to save his soul. This grief left pain in his mother like a sharp knife that twisted her throat. The youngest sister, Ha, closed her eyes to reduce the pain. She remembered her brother with respect and her memories. The death of Kiet had to be recognized; his dreams of finding his father had vanished. Who would justify all of this? He once existed in this world and what was left? A young Amerasian death unknown! He lay there, a cold corpse, eyes wide open. I gently closed his eyes with my hand. I remembered the first two days in the USA. He took my family to Penn's Landing to take a picture with us. I remembered the times we spent at the testing center for school. In high school, he took my English exam paper and copied it. Luckily, our teacher didn't catch him. I was really upset with him. In spite of his silliness, I liked him all the same. I appreciated his kindness and his willingness. I realized, *A life without a friend, the world without the sunlight.*

Kiet's death brought me some closure. I had thought I had been swindled by ideas that were fragile, like the morning dew on weeds would be melted by the heat of the sun, and then the dew becomes a firm substance. (I meant our accidental meeting in this life.) In this world, we usually honor one another because of our energy and how our values are measured by it.

As human beings, we cannot live without feelings. Sentiment plays a very important role in human life, but people do not know the value of noble sentiment until they lose it. I have become a compassionate person toward human beings. I know I have to be recognized as fully human like other living beings. The more I think about human life, the more I love the person who is suffering in this life because I have been there. I cannot debase myself to ask for any pity. I thought those who have the most virtue in their words have the least of it in their bosom because virtue must be clarified by action, not by speech. I also realized that there are no forces that can overcome fate, but I must at least show my courage. "Lost money is something. Lost love is a major loss. But when you lose courage, you lose everything." I gathered all of my abilities for gaining something in this world, sweet world, melodious sound, nobility of communion, and so forth, but all of my abilities are transformed by the dregs of this world.

My mother and I went to the Concept Beauty Academy School for Cosmetology. During the daytime, I attended college, and I went to training at the career school in the evening. It was rough for four months, but it was worth it for a lifetime. My mother seemed to struggle in learning, but with my help, she gained some knowledge in school. We both passed the exam and became licensed manicurists. My mother opened a nail shop soon after.

My half-sisters and I had lovely summer times together. We played jump rope, shot water guns, shopped for new Barbies. Even though there was a difference in age, they were still good company for me. We found a dog around the bar while walking home. At first, my mother refused to let us keep the dog. We left the dog outside the house for a couple of nights; no one came to identify the dog. It sat patiently, waiting for us. We named her Lien Lien. She was the funniest Chihuahua we had ever seen. We loved to walk the dog in the late evening. Lien Lien always ran ahead of us, poking her nose into every corner she found on the way. She was so excited that she barked at everyone and wagged her tail all the way home. We loved giving our dog a manicure to match her outfit. Lien was our knockout beauty princess doggy.

My father dropped me off after a visit with my grandmother. We rang the bell for a while; finally, my stepfather opened the door. We stepped inside the house and said hello to my mother. She appeared upset toward us.

"Where did you take my daughter?" she said sternly to my father.

My father replied, "We came back here late last night. We rang the bell for more than a half-hour, and the rain began to pour, so we headed back to my mother's home."

My mother didn't seem to listen to my father's explanation, and she started a fight with him. I tried to call the police, but my stepfather felt it would be better to call our sponsor at church. Around fifteen minutes later, she came to the house. She used Bible teaching to lecture my father. My father disagreed with her advice and said, "God has a power to bring people together, or he can separate them when he feels they are in danger."

She gave up trying to convince my father. She told my mother that this American man had a loud mouth.

I was so upset at her. I told her to please not mess up my family by giving us a false thoughts. I translated to my father about what she had just said. My father said, "Let God bless her, please."

My father left the house. I was completely heartbroken. I didn't feel anything but anger. I started to feel sorry for my mother. The story of a painful episode from my past rolling in front of my eyes, I began to cry. A twenty-two-year-old girl, frightened, not daring to acknowledge I didn't even know who I was. My thoughts wandered toward the events of the past year that had reshaped my life. I wondered, *Mommy, did you ever love me?* I was in denial and was hoping for things to change. I felt like an animal, afraid of her; the other half of me still loved her. That night, my thoughts were so empty, and I wished the moonlight would steal me away.

The next day, my father called to comfort me. I told him I was sorry about what had happened at my house. My father told me, "At least I experienced some of the pain you have been going through for so many years." He advised me to do well in school, and he would be proud of my accomplishment in so short a time in the United States. I promised my father I would be somebody one day. Regardless of whatever they called me, using unkind words to destroy my character, I had to work extra hard to be a success.

I joined the International Festival during the New Year at the Community College of Philadelphia. I was dancing with a group of Vietnamese students. We went to Canada for the best performance in silk dance and fan dance. My mother was not very happy about this.

One day, after I'd had one of many fights with my mother, my boyfriend found me in the saddest state. School was over, but I had no interest in going home. I had extremely mixed emotions on the train. I felt anger, sadness, and betrayal chasing me like a cycle, a cycle of suffering. I sat in the train and let the train take me as if on an endless journey.

Then, late at night, I was hungry, with no money, no personal items, nothing at all. I realized I had to get off the train to look for shelter for the night. I was at the 69th Street Station in Upper Darby. I saw the homeless were everywhere at the bus station. I had a panic attack thinking that I had to stay there. I was worried about getting robbed, raped, and assaulted. Anything could happen on the street. I quickly opened my schoolbook bag to get the number of one of my friends who had just got married and lived around there. I was so thankful they let me come over.

I spent almost two weeks at their place to finish my final exams. I got very good grades in my exams. Every night, I tried to get home late to avoid dinner.

I passed by the beautiful stores that were decorated for Christmas and the New Year. The colors of the Christmas lights, the people holding hands on the sidewalk, the jingle-bell song--all reminded people that it was time to unite with the family. I left my home when people got ready to celebrate a New Year. I had nowhere to call home. I had sympathy for those homeless people who were unlucky. *Please be sorry for those who are unlucky,* I prayed.

Two week passed. I survived with some help from my Vietnamese friends and my boyfriend. I found an apartment located close to Temple University School of Pharmacy in Philadelphia. I shared a room with three Vietnamese pharmacy students who had come there from different cities to study. My boyfriend helped me through this difficult time. He went with me looking for my new apartment. We rang the doorbell. My new roommates welcomed us with great enthusiasm. It gave me a good impression. They offered to help me carry my personal items into the apartment. I told them I didn't have anything except the half-full trash bag of old clothes my girlfriend had given me and fifty dollars her mother had given me for lucky New Year. She had won a big card game the last night I was there.

The following day, my roommates took me around the city to find a job. I saw a new Vietnamese restaurant that had just opened. I wrote the number down to apply for a job. The next day, I got accepted for a waitress job. In the daytime, I was a full-time student at the community college; in the evening, I worked until midnight. I saved some money for the rent. I paid only one hundred and fifty dollars and saved some money for college. I got good tips at Christmas and New Year's by singing karaoke. I learned to be self-reliant. On New Year's Eve, I called my grandmother to wish her Happy New Year. I told my father I was okay and working hard. My father encouraged me to be strong and move on like a new transition. I began fighting for my independence and created my own way to live in this world. At the end of that year, I graduated with an associate's degree in gerontology; I invited my mother's family and my father to attend the graduation. I introduced my boyfriend to everyone. My father greeted him with a big hug. After the ceremony, we said good-bye to each other in a civilized manner.

— —

I heard the voices of thousands of abused children who cried softly, innocent children who every day were abused by their family members, struggling to survive through physiological and psychological turmoil. No one could erase all of the torture of anguish and pain that caused their innocent souls to become an angry sea.

The unforgettable stories of my patients at the Philadelphia Child Guidance Center of the Children's Hospital broke my heart.

A little Hispanic girl cried, "Please don't hurt me." She was transferred from the Children's Hospital's burn unit and placed in the observation room to be supervised by a doctor, nurse, psychiatric counselor, and physical therapist. She had second-degree burns. The right side of her body and her arms were swollen, and her skin tissue was red and extremely sensitive. I was assigned to be her counselor.

She was a small girl with long black hair and black eyes. She was ten years old and had been abused by her foster parents. They had tried to kill her by drowning her in a hot bathtub. She somehow had lived through the ordeal. She had difficulty engaging with the staff in the unit. The horrible experience with her foster parents had traumatized her. The nurses had to apply oil cream on her burned skin. She was scared to go to the bathroom and take a bath.

I wanted to learn from this girl as well as to educate her. It would help me to relate to my patients and show her genuine concern and empathy. The most important thing for me was to help her stay focused in her physical therapy sessions. I taught her how to build her self-esteem and her trust level. In a couple of months, she showed phenomenal progress. She grew stronger and found the strength to live again. Her foster parents got locked up because of their abuse of her.

Who could not have fallen in love with a little six-year-old Hispanic boy. He was there because his mother had abandoned him at a young age; he had some difficulty following directions and obeying authority. Overall, he was a cute little boy. He spent almost a year at the Child Guidance Center, before he got accepted to go to the Spring Hill center. On his discharge day, I took him and some of his peers to the cafeteria. He looked so sad. I reached out and hugged him. He squeezed my hand so tightly, and I had the feeling there was deep emotion behind the words he was trying to say. I told him how special he was and reminded him how far he had come. That night, I went to say good-bye to him. He stood there and sobbed. I ran out the door. It was the last time I saw my little boy.

After a long day of therapeutic sessions and schooling, when night fell, all of the children needed their loved ones. They became tearful or acted out with negative behavior. The children came from the north and south of the city, from the suburbs, and from placement centers. They were white, black, Hispanic, Asian. What these innocent children had endured was truly beyond imagining. They never knew love; they experienced all of the feelings of pain and humiliation. Like everyone, they thirsted for love and needed comfort, compassion, food, clothing, and shelter. They needed a place to have a safe night to sleep and hide from the sun or rain.

On the day I became a citizen of the USA, I had butterflies in my stomach--not that I was nervous, just excited. I had been waiting for this moment, to be a legal citizen living in America. America is the land of freedom and opportunity. As an Amerasian, I share in the greatest of the American home, sweet home. How I wanted to live here. The Constitution of this land depended very much on God, and even the money said, "In God we trust." It meant everything to me.

On December 16, 1996, my father gave me his last name. Pham Ngoc Anh, my Vietnamese name, became Angelina Wentz. It was a miracle day that welcomed me to a life without torment.

The most recent bill regarding Amerasians in the United States and in Asia is the Amerasian Naturalization Act of 2003. It has been in the legislative process, and it seems like it is not going to pass. American law does not consider Amerasians as citizens by birth, even though their fathers are American. Congressman James Moran,

Virginia Democrat, has played a large part in the effort to permit Amerasians to become US citizens automatically. I couldn't agree more with Congressman Moran. This was sending a message of hope to Amerasians who are living in the USA, struggling to survive in a culture that mixed heritage and abandonment. At least they would know they were accepted by their fatherland. I appreciate and applaud those involved in fighting for Amerasians' rights. I wish that one day, not so far away, justice will be realized.

In 1996, Philadelphia was drowning in a snowstorm. The entire city was shut down because of more than twenty-two inches of snow. I was lying in my apartment and thinking about the children at the Child Guidance Center. I called in to check on the staff and the children. The whole facility was short on staff and needed help. I didn't hesitate and got ready to walk to the Children's Hospital, ten blocks away.

The cold air swept over my body. My face was red, and my fingers were numb. I tried to bury my face deeper into the scarf around my neck, but the cold air would not relent. My feet were buried deeper in snow with every step I took. I ended up falling in the snow. No one was outside on the street, not even the trucks that clear the snow. The whole city became a white wonderland. The wind was picking up from every direction, and I was alone in the desert of snow. The frost bit my ears; the snow fell on my face. The chilling wind blew right though my body and I felt like my skin was cracking. The only thing I could think of was getting to my patients. I imagined they were waiting for me, and I was coming. Here I fell, there I picked myself up, and slowly, with every baby step I walked, I could hear the children calling for me. I felt brave and had more reason to keep going. When my feet almost gave up on me, I tried to walk as fast as my legs could carry me. I was already getting cramps throughout my body, and I was still a few blocks away. I gathered all of my strength to walk through the snow. My feet were drenched from the puddles of the deep snow. I pulled myself through the horrible blizzard.

When I turned the key to open the door, all of the staff and the patients welcomed me with open arms. The children ran to hug me. They gave me a blanket to keep warm. My makeup was smeared from the wet snow; the mascara messed up my eyes so that I looked like a clown. The pinching cold air made my face swollen. My patients seemed to love me even more. I took tremendous satisfaction from my patients. I worked a double shift that week. At night, I stayed at the Penn Tower Hotel across from the Children's Hospital.

The president of the hospital was very grateful that I showed up in a crucial time of crisis and wrote me a letter:

PHILADELPHIA CHILD GUIDANCE CENTER
ADMINISTRATION
MEMORANDUM

TO: Anh Pham
FROM: Jerome M. Gibbs, Ph.D.
President and Chief Executive Officer
DATE: January 11, 1996
SUBJECT: KUDOS! ACCOLADES!

I want to personally thank you for your loyalty, dedication, and commitment to the children of PCGC and for the time that you put in during the Blizzard of 1996. Without hesitation, you saw a need and fulfilled it, and for that PCGC is truly grateful. Your display of enthusiasm and team spirit is exemplary. Your assistance was crucial to the survival of our children and, again, I say thank you and send my gratitude.

In 1997, I went to Temple University for a social work major. I did an internship at the Department of Veterans Affairs Medical Center, assigned to Ward 5 West under the supervision of nursing service personnel on the ward. The agency works with retired veterans who are on disability. Many of them served in the Korean War and the Vietnam War. So, I became interested in how the US. government treats its senior citizen servicemen.

I had mixed emotions. There were aspects of the program that were very helpful and that met the needs of the senior citizens. During my practicum, I learned a great deal about soldiers and how brave they were by sacrificing for their country. These brave soldiers fought for their country, lost their limbs, and lost their sense of well-being. Even though they were physically handicapped, they had excellent mental abilities. Thousands and thousand of soldiers who served in Vietnam were exposed to the poison called Agent Orange, which was a chemical herbicide that may have exposed them to cancer, skin disease, and other side effects. In Vietnam, there is a song about the poison of orange skin: "The poison orange was killing my innocent darling. It was the orange poison destroyed my baby's face..."

I accrued a total of five hundred hours of volunteer service to veterans and was a welcome addition to the

Medical Center at the VA Hospital. A group of people and I were recognized as excellent volunteers. Mayor Ed Rendell presented the award. He was a great supporter of the VA Hospital.

— —

In 1968, my father was in the US Army, stationed at Nha Trang in Vietnam. He specialized in radio communication and transportation. I am so proud of my father, and I feel a strong sense of pride and respect for veterans. The tradition of the military is to fight fairly and honorably. My father said his service in the US military was his choice. It seemed the right thing to do for his country. The idea of American democracy is to help people in need. The Vietnam War will always be remembered as a human tragedy for those who lived and died in the conflict. He said the worst thing was that there was no frontline fight with the Communist soldiers. The Army gave him the tools and core beliefs that guided him for the rest of his life. The war may have been a military loss, he said, but it was a great victory for the human race and the meaning of human dignity and nobility.

Because of the war, my father had some difficulty readjusting and relieving his anxiety. He joined a program in Lebanon, Pennsylvania, under the care of Dr. Justin in 1980. The years seemed to have slipped by and caught him unaware that faith had not allowed his power of thought to be paralyzed. In 1989, when I finally was reunited with my father, we shared our life experiences and learned how to cope with them, helping each other to heal the pain.

Shortly after I met my father, I met my Uncle Bernie. I spoke with him briefly about the Vietnam War. Our conversation brought back many memories for him, some good and some not so good. He was born and raised with strict family values. He learned to respect others, to be kind to the environment, and to be a good citizen. He volunteered for a tour of duty in the Marine Corps after he graduated from college with a BS degree in June of 1966. After completing basic training and advanced infantry training, he was placed in aviation supply school. Following his schooling, because of his achievements, he was given a choice of duty stations, and he chose WESTPAC, which at the time was Vietnam. Thirteen months was the normal tour of duty in Vietnam for the Marines. His first duty station was with Marine Air Group 36, a helicopter unit at Tam Ky, north of Chu Lai, Vietnam, and he arrived there on or about December 22, 1966. In the summer of 1967, his unit moved farther north to a place called Phu Bai, which is near the city of Hue, after the Army took over the base at Tam Ky. Generally, the Marine Corps carried out its operations in the I Corps area, which was the northernmost corps area in South Vietnam. He spent two Christmases in Vietnam prior to coming home January 1968.

The military in general and the Vietnam War specifically taught him to be alert and always be aware of what was going on around him, but much more important, he felt it taught him the need to be able to communicate and get along with people. Living with the same group of people, all day, every day, and generally in difficult conditions, seemed to bring out the worst in people. It seemed that short of overlooking immoral behavior or illegal acts, he had to basically learn to accept other people's shortcomings while at the same time being aware of his own behavior and how it affected other people, in order to avoid conflicts.

Regarding the legitimacy of the war, his personal views

were that our country was there to help people and to prevent them from being ruled, against their will, by a Communist government. In any case, he left the decisions about Vietnam up to the nation's leaders. He felt that everyone should do what he could, within the system, to put the proper people in power for running the country and government, and then be able to continue to voice their opinions. However, no one should object individually to the point that he could flee the country during wartime, if he intended to return following the war. He felt strongly that anyone who fled and wanted to return should be required to do a minimum of two years of work in some civil capacity upon return. That would be in addition to being charged with any specific crimes committed by fleeing. He felt the country should act as one, and individuals should not be allowed to reap the benefits of a free society but be allowed to flee during difficult times, only to return when things got better.

Although he spent time at night on guard duty on the perimeter of his base, spent time in the jungle at night on six-man listening posts, monitoring enemy activity, and rode as a security gunner on truck convoys during supply deliveries to outposts, he felt he was much luckier than many other Marines, who spent a large part of their time during their tour of duty in continuous direct combat. He had volunteered for the Marine Corps, for Vietnam, and for many other activities while in Vietnam, as he felt it was the right thing to do and, to some degree, because he was looking for adventure.

Upon his return, he was not really aware that there wasn't a "hero's welcome" as there was at the conclusion of other wars, and to some degree, that may have been because individuals were continuously volunteering or being inducted into the Armed Services, and eventually being deployed, while troops were constantly being released from active duty during the same period of time, even though the war was not officially over until the mid-1970s. He accepted the experience as his responsibility, just by virtue of being a male in a "free society," where, contrary to what many uninformed people think, everything is not free, but in fact must be paid for. One of the most difficult and demoralizing experiences he had to contend with while he was overseas were the public demonstrations against the government by its own people, which he felt appeared all too often on news programs. In any case, in the absence of any physical reminders and with only some bad memories to deal with, upon his release he eagerly moved ahead with his life. He felt friends, family, and really anyone he interacted with following his return treated him very well.

<hr />

For so many years, I had been dreaming of the things that would make my life a little better, more desirable or more beautiful, someone I could call my own, my lover, and my companion for life. Tasweer and I met in the first year of college. Seven years later, he asked me to marry him. I was so happy. My father was very pleased with my choice. On the other hand, my mother seemed hesitant to accept him as a son-in-law. My stepfather tried to prevent me from marrying him. He told me my future husband, a Pakistani, was Muslim and would get married to five wives. I had already made up my mind to marry him. We had been through so much with each other. He was always there for me, believing in me and lifting my spirits when I was blue.

——

May 9, 1998, was a special day in my life. After so many years of waiting, it was finally time for us to get married. We had a lovely wedding in a hotel restaurant in New Jersey. I dressed just like an Indian movie star, with a ruby-red wedding dress and jewelry from head to toe. I felt so special and beautiful that night. I can still remember the wedding as if it just happened yesterday. There was a DJ playing the music and nonstop dancing. A group of professional dancers came to cheer our wedding night. My father gave me away with a lot of pride. My uncle and his wife traveled many miles to attend our wedding. My mother, my stepfather, and two of my half-sisters came to the wedding, even though there were bittersweet memories between my mother and me. I appreciated and was thankful my mother was there, and especially that my Amerasian friend Tuan was there for our special day. He was truly a friend. "A friend in need is a friend indeed." The wedding day is always vivid in my mind. I was so thrilled with the man I love, and I cherish him deeply.

——

I did an internship at Friends Hospital of Philadelphia. I planned my work in order to become a professional social worker. I accomplished this by working with clients on all levels, to ensure that my clients were knowledgeable about all of the resources available to them and to fight for those who were not. In group therapy on loss and grief, I helped them to talk and express their feelings as well as help them to heal their emotional scars so that they might move on with their lives. I also participated in all group therapies, such as psychotherapy, anger management, depression, self-esteem, and focus groups. Finally, I had several meetings with my supervisor, Mr. David Como, deputy director for community programs, to discuss issues regarding mental illness treatment at Friends Hospital and what its purpose is and what the main goal in helping the clients was for us. His passion, dedication, and vision have served the clients' needs. He is a brilliant man.

Friends Hospital was a great opportunity because it taught me about the exceptional diversity of people. We are all faced with the future. Human beings need motivation to help them to continue to do well. We have made the community more aware of mental health problems present in our society. The more I realized that, the more I expanded my work beyond just the book. I now understand them and acknowledge them as regular people just like us needing help. I became sensitive to the ways in which I affected other people and the ways in which people affected me. My heart melted with awareness of the human struggle and human openness toward this universe. I am not alone!

—◆—

Nowhere would I have rather spent my time studying than at the Tuttleman Learning Center of Temple University. This remarkable high-tech building gave students greater access to the modern world. The building was recently built, and we had an open house in October of 1999. I was so excited to see Governor Tom Ridge. He walked though the building and shook my hand and wished me luck with school. I had lots of respect and admiration for Governor Ridge because of his enthusiasm toward Amerasians' homecoming. I really wanted to tell him who I was, but time was limited. It was a nice surprise to see such an important person.

— —

Perhaps no word is more expressive than "graduated." I didn't think it would happen to me. The thought passed by me like an animated image. This was my American dream! As I look into the past, I am convinced that everything I've ever completed was quite worth it. I refused to stay still and accept my misfortune. I fully recognized I had to fight for my destiny. Education was the key to open my future because society recognizes knowledge and intelligence are important.

I was inspired by my instructor, Dr. Ruth Gillman at Temple University of Philadelphia. She was my inspiration. She taught me enthusiastically, so I gained a lot of knowledge from her. She was very strict and firm at times. The philosophy Dr. Ruth used as a teacher in senior seminar was realistic. She demonstrated some techniques to educate students so they can get ready to confront the real world. (For example, we all can strive to be like a lighthouse, guiding others to safety by consistently shining our internal light, no matter what else is going on around us.) She was a model educator I will always admire.

The graduation music began, and as the band continued to play, I was enthralled by the experience. It was life's best moment for the students, with the farewell from the university president and, especially, the speaker, Dr. Bill Cosby, who starred in *The Cosby Show* on television. We were honored to have him on graduation day. The class of 2000!

For so many years, I tried to work on my emotions because of the abandonment of Amerasian children in Vietnamese society and the problems between me and my mother and my stepfather. The fights with my mother, in my dreams, were aggressive and came often. She was the woman who gave birth to me, and yet in some ways there was so much distance between us. The damage in our relationship could not be undone. I willingly tried to be close to her, but every time we stepped closer together, we seemed to push each other further and further away. How much I missed my mother being involved in my life before my stepfather stepped into our lives. My life was very much living on the edge and staring into the abyss, as long as I didn't slip and fall.

Recently, I spoke with my close cousin, Tuyet, who was my mother's favorite niece. My cousin was very aware of everything about my life situation. In my stillness, I shared with my cousin what was happening in my current life, with the worst nightmares coming back and haunting me. I jumped up in the bed in the middle of the night and stared out the window, losing my mind in the shadow of the dimmed light across the street. I thought, *Am I hallucinating or did I just wake up from a bad dream?*

Then, those sad memories of my life started rolling in my mind. With a pen in my hand, I could reach places where no voice could ever reach. For so many years, I tried to bury and block the terrible memories from my mind. Suddenly, those memories all came back and suffocated me. All I did was cry; tears helped mend the wounds in me and made my heart heal. Even now, every time I look in the mirror, I still see a little girl, crying and being so vulnerable.

The sadness, the anger kept following me like a dark shadow, and I had to be willing to confront my own truth- -my lonely buried secrets about to be released and revealed. I'd feel guilty, and I couldn't do anything to save my soul. The guilt of reliving the sad story of my family swept over me. I was so disappointed, but I tried anyway. I couldn't leave myself in darkness forever, and I wanted to be free.

One night, my daughter was acting out. I put her outside the garage door just for a few minutes. I felt so terrible, I realized I don't have the heart to see the tears in my child's eyes. My exhausted feeling was killing me inside. I was so tense, tearful, and depressed. I didn't lose faith to pray for a miracle to free me. I couldn't control my emotional distress, so I started to write.

My mother stopped talking to me after my second child's first birthday because she felt I treated my in-laws with more respect than her family. I couldn't believe it. It couldn't be further from the truth. I could not control what she was thinking, but in my heart I felt I had done everything a daughter could do for her mother. One part of me will never stop believing that one day my mother will come to her senses when it's not too late. Because I do love her!

＊＊

As I look back, forgotten actions come again to haunt me. The further I went into life, the gloomier I felt. It was almost yesterday that I could not recall showing any interest in the world. It was as though the world was filled with obscenities, and no matter which way I turned, all that existed was stupid and debasing cruelty. Religion and worship meant nothing to me, only hollow and empty thoughts. Long wishful thinking with no one to love left me with the drive to discover the truth. I came to realize the existence of God. However, I had yet to discover my purpose. That part of my life was a difficult task. I had something to do, something to learn, a need to matter and to be self-confident about the correct way to do it. Despite all of the hurt I was dealing with. I would like to ease many things from my past. Growing up in a dysfunctional home makes me so sad. As a result, I have many scars in my heart. In the process, out of my bad childhood, I felt something wonderful happened. I wanted to be a therapist to work with children who were abused or who had to deal with a life-trauma, felt unwanted and misplaced. I didn't want to give up. I came out stronger to face everyday life. I am the same person, unchangeable, loyal and patient.

———

I am an Amerasian who arrived in the United States on August 2, 1989. As an Amerasian in Vietnam, I was perceived as inferior throughout my childhood and up until now. At the time I left my home country, I was constantly mocked and alienated. Through I have endured much, I have managed to retain my humanity and compassion, as a survivor of both mental and physical discrimination. I wish to share my story to heal others and myself. I hope this story will overcome the obstacles that are keeping me from becoming who I really am and to be for my fellow Amerasians a voice to be heard. From the bottom of my heart, I dedicate this story to more than fifty thousand Amerasian children who faced a very similar fate--prejudice and rejection, abandoned, unwanted, and isolated. Their pain is no different from my pain! We are all the same as humans!

The light of my soul was nearly extinguished. But as each day passes, I notice myself stronger and bolder. I feel the healing of the wounds within me. I must prove to myself that I know the true and the right, and how glad I will be to remain faithful to myself. In my deepest distress, I requested guidance in a most deceiving yet scared world. I wondered if my fantasy would become reality. Perhaps one day, I would be able to deal with my personal experiences. Experience and knowledge kindled my life with gratification, deep self-trust, and courage in the face of difficulty in my lifetime. Those scary days, lonely and sad memories, as well as happy memories, are part of my life, of who am I, an Amerasian. As time goes on and the years go by, I gather belief that after a while, all of us start to forget our lives. Amerasians' lives were shattered, wretchedly. No word of accepting, just plain wonderment. With the conviction that all of us are entitled to lead our lives the way we wanted. My despair turned at once to gladness, which did not force me to struggle through the lonely years against the indignities and frustrations forced upon me. My mind tried to forget, but my heart still burns.

For several years, I went through some real soul-searching. My renewed thoughts through values were dedication and moral principles of what I am to become encouraged my soul. That is a reason for me to survive the difficult times. To all of my fellow Amerasian brothers and sisters around the world: We feel great pain and anger when our possessions are destroyed. Amerasian identity is very important to all of our next generation and us. The only true justification for our different life is our choice to do so. Let's not blame destiny or fate for our own race, but, most important, feel a sense of who we are, then to learn to overcome the struggles, obstacles, and barriers that would encounter our life in a long term of process. Despite all of the heartaches, discrimination, many images of our life float into our troubled mind. The best thing that came out of it is that we can pointedly talk about goals, skill survival because Amerasians are wonderful people. Once I can define my race, one half Vietnamese and another half American, I can be proud. How long do we have to wait to be accepted by society? It was a beautiful feeling to accept who I am and who we are. Let people recognize the Amerasian existence.

THE END

Breinigsville, PA USA
26 October 2010
248044BV00004B/19/P